VIRAT KOHLI

© B. Jain Publishers (P) Ltd. All rights reserved. No part of this book may be reproduced, stored in a retrieval system or transmitted, in any form or by any means, mechanical, photocopying, recording or otherwise, without any prior written permission of the publisher.

Published by Kuldeep Jain for B. Jain Publishers (P) Ltd., D-157, Sector 63, Noida - 201307, U.P
Registered office: 1921/10, Chuna Mandi, Paharganj, New Delhi-110055

Printed in India

Contents

5	Who is Virat Kohli?
8	Childhood and Inspirations
16	Early Cricket Life
26	Breakthrough in the Indian National Cricket Team
36	International Cricket
46	Team Player and Captaincy
62	Personal Strengths and Overcoming Challenges
72	Personal Life
73	Records, Awards and Recognition
75	Timeline
77	Activities
79	Glossary

Who is Virat Kohli?

Virat Kohli is a very talented and popular Indian cricketer. He has been awarded the prestigious Arjuna Award for Sports by the President of India. In 2014, he became the captain of the Indian cricket team for Test Cricket. At the time he was the vice-captain of the team for limited-overs matches, including One-Day International (ODI) and Twenty20 (T20) matches, since 2012. However, in early 2017, he was appointed the captain of the national cricket team in limited-overs format as well.

Virat is a right-handed batsman. He is also a good medium-pace bowler and an energetic, athletic fielder. Virat was part of the Indian cricket Team that won the ICC Cricket World Cup in 2011. He is also the top rated T20 cricket player in the world, according to the ICC rankings.

Apart from playing for the Indian National Team, Kohli is also part of the Indian Premier League

(IPL). Here, he is the Captain of the Royal Challengers Bangalore Team, which he has led since 2013.

Kohli is about 5 feet 9 inches tall (175 cm), and has a forceful and competitive style of playing. Though he has always shown great passion for the game, over the years, he has become more level headed and mature. He is well-known for playing very well under pressure situations.

Other than cricket, he enjoys video games, tennis and football. Roger Federer is one of his favourite tennis players and his favourite cricket player is Sachin Tendulkar.

Childhood and Inspirations

Virat was born in New Delhi on 5th November 1988. He grew up in a average middle-class Punjabi household in New Delhi. He was the youngest of three siblings—he has an older brother, Vikash and an elder sister, Bhavna.

His father, Prem Kohli, was a criminal lawyer, while his mother, Saroj Kohli, was a stay-at-home parent. His parents, especially his father, had a very strong influence on young Virat. Even today, he is very close to his family. The Kohlis lived in Uttam Nagar in West Delhi, where Virat attended Vishal Bharti Public School.

Virat always dreamt of playing cricket. Even as a three-year-old toddler, his favourite game was to take up his small bat, while his father would bowl for him. As he grew older, he started playing cricket in the by lanes of his locality with other children. In fact, one of his earliest childhood memories is of playing gully cricket with his friends, using tennis balls. Even though he had no training

at the time, he was a very good batsman. That is the reason that everyone who saw him play at that age thought he was very talented. They all advised his father to help him develop his natural talent. Virat's father too recognised that his son had a rare natural ability, and always supported him. He would push him to practise every day, and taught him to never give up.

Virat also loved watching cricket on TV, and always tried to copy the batsmen's shots. He was a fan of Sachin Tendulkar, and loved watching him play. As he has said, "Sachin is someone who has inspired me immensely. Just watching him play for India, I used to dream of winning games for India, because he used to do it single handedly.

He has been my superhero and he will be that for my lifetime."

The West Delhi Cricket Academy was formed in 1998. Virat was nine years old, when his father enrolled him in the first batch. This was the first time that Virat started learning proper techniques, rather than relying on his own natural game.

Virat's coach at the academy, Rajkumar Sharma, also had a strong influence on him. In fact, it was his coach who gave young Virat his nickname, 'Cheeku'. He too encouraged Virat to stay fit and practise the game every day.

When he was in class nine, Virat shifted schools. He now joined Saviour Convent in Paschim Vihar, to help with his cricket practise. However, he did not ignore his studies. He was intelligent and studied hard. His teachers say that he was a "bright and alert child".

Early Cricket Life

In 2002, while he was still in school, Kohli was selected to play for the Delhi Under-15 team for the Polly Umrigar Trophy. He was not even 14 years old, but he was the leading run scorer. The following year, he was selected as the Captain of the Delhi U-15 team for the same competition.

In 2004, Kohli was selected for the Delhi Under-17 team to play for the 2003-2004 Vijay Merchant Trophy. The very next year, he was the highest run-scorer in the tournament, which his team won. As a result, he was selected for the India Under-19 squad in July 2006. This gave him an opportunity to play outside India as well.

On the U-19 tour of England, he played in both ODIs and test matches. He played well in all the matches, and consistently scored runs. The team won both the ODI and Test matches in this series. During the tour, Virat impressed the India U-19 coach, Lalchand Rajput, who said

that his batting showed "strong technical skills" against both pace and spin bowling.

Later that year, in November 2006, Kohli made his debut in first-class cricket, playing for Delhi. In December, he was playing for Delhi against the Karnataka team, when

his father passed away. His father had suffered a brain stroke and had been unwell for a month. When Kohli learnt of his father's death, he was at the crease. Instead of rushing home, he chose to complete his innings. He made 90 runs, before he was dismissed. He went directly to the funeral from the match.

The Delhi coach and his teammates were touched as well as impressed by Virat Kohli's commitment to the team. This match marked a huge shift in Kohli's outlook and attitude. He recalls, "The way I approached the game changed that day. I just had one thing in my mind—that I have to play for my country and live that dream for my dad."

Kohli's mother, too, noted the change in her son. She said that he became much more mature as a person. "It was as if his life hinged totally on cricket after that day," she said. With his greatest inspiration gone, he was playing not just for himself, but also to fulfil his father's dreams.

After completing his schooling, Kohli did not apply for college. Instead, his focus on cricket became even more intense. As a result of his good performance, he was appointed the Indian Team Captain for the 2008 U-19 Cricket World Cup, held in Malaysia. He was overall the third highest run-scorer of the tournament, and was awarded two 'Man of the Match' trophies. The team won the U-19 World Cup, and Virat Kohli quickly became a player to watch out for.

Later that same year, Kohli was picked for the India Emerging Players Squad for the four-team Emerging

Players Tournament held in Australia. He maintained his good form throughout, and it was no surprise when he was noticed by the selectors of the Indian National Cricket Team.

Breakthrough in the Indian National Cricket Team

The Indian team selectors recognised Kohli's potential, and included him in the Indian ODI squad in August 2008. However, he had to prove himself time and again before he could win a permanent place in the squad.

Kohli made his international debut during the Indian tour of Sri Lanka in 2008 at the age of 19. Over the next several months, Kohli was called to play at any position that opened in the batting line-up, to replace injured players.

In July-August 2009, Kohli played in the Emerging Players Tournament in Australia. Here, he was the leading run-scorer, helping his team to victory time and time again.

Krishnamachari Srikkanth was the Chairman of the National Selection Committee at the time, and noted that Kohli had a lot of ability. In fact, he said that Kohli had been "outstanding" in the tournament as an opener. Kohli himself believes this tournament marked a turning point in his career.

Kohli was given a place in the team for the December 2009 home ODI series against Sri Lanka. It was during the fourth match that he scored 107 off 111 balls—his first ODI century. India won the match and the series. Although Gautam Gambhir was awarded the Man of the Match Award, he gave it to Kohli, as he felt Kohli deserved it.

Kohli then played in the January 2010 tri-nation ODI Tournament in Bangladesh. He played well consistently, and secured his second ODI century. He thus became only the third Indian batsman to have scored two ODI centuries before their twenty second birthday. Kohli also emerged as the leading

run-scorer of the series. His performance was praised by all, especially by the then Indian Captain, MS Dhoni.

During the summer of 2010, several major Indian players were unable to play in the Tri-series Tournament in

Zimbabwe. As a result, Suresh Raina was named the captain and Kohli was made the vice-captain for the series. Virat became the fastest Indian to score 1,000 runs in ODIs. However, despite his excellent performance, India lost the series.

After this, Kohli went through a bad patch, where he could not perform well. Kohli's poor performance in the matches created a lot of pressure on him. However, he never gave up, and kept practising and improving his game. His effort paid off, and in late 2010, Kohli played brilliantly when India played against New Zealand. He

scored a century and two half-centuries, and displayed his excellent team work skills through his partnerships with Gautam Gambhir. India defeated New Zealand 5-0 in the series, and Kohli was confirmed as a regular member of the team.

During 2010, Kohli emerged as the highest ODI run-scorer in the Indian cricket team—he scored 995 runs in just 25 matches, including three centuries. He was on the way to achieving his dream.

International Cricket

The year 2011 started out as a good year for Kohli. He was part of the South African tour, where India won the T20 tournament. Though India lost the ODI series, Kohli once again emerged as the top scorer within the team. He

also reached the number 2 spot on the ICC rankings for ODI batsmen.

Kohli was then included in the 15-man Indian squad for the ICC Cricket World Cup. In the very first match, he scored an unbeaten 100, becoming the first Indian to score a century on his World Cup debut. Kohli played in every

match of the World Cup, and even though his scores dropped in some of the matches, he contributed in the final as a team player by putting up a valuable partnership with Gautam Gambhir. This led to India winning the World Cup for the first time since 1983. This was a very proud moment for Kohli and the entire team.

Apart from the professional success that he was now slowly gaining, this period was also exciting for Kohli for another reason. Having watched cricket since he was a child, it was a dream come true for him to not only meet, but to get to know several legendary cricketers, such as Sachin Tendulkar, as his team mates and friends. During the 2011 World Cup, Kohli said, "Sachin Tendulkar has carried the burden of the nation for 21 years. It is time we carried him on our shoulders."

Later that same year, Kohli finally got the chance to play Test cricket match for the country.

In Test cricket, a single match continues for 3-5 days at a time. It is considered to be much more tiring for the

players, and needs a more mature style of playing. Kohli made his Test debut at Kingston against the West Indies, but struggled to perform in this format. It was not until October 2011, that he found his pace in Test cricket matches and scored the highest number of runs during England's tour of India, where India won 5-0.

At the end of 2011, Kohli was selected as part of the Indian Test team that toured Australia. The series started off slow, and Kohli was not able to find his feet. In the second Test in Sydney, he lost his temper at the crowd while fielding. As a result, the match referee fined him. However, his overall performance and attitude improved

in the next match, he scored his maiden Test century in the fourth and final Test match. Even though India lost the

series, Kohli's effort was seen as the "lone bright spot" in an otherwise terrible tour for the Indian team.

The same pattern was seen in the ODI games that followed. Kohli remained focused and played consistently well throughout. His aggressive and competitive style of playing served to rejuvenate and pep up the entire team.

Kohli was once again India's highest run scorer and the only one to score a century in the series.

Virat's repeated high scores and competitive presence on the field led him once again to emerge as the top scorer in ODIs in 2011.

Team Player and Captaincy

The Indian team may not have done well in Australia, but Kohli's steady form and obvious capability was noted by all. Krishnamachari Srikkanth, the then chairman of selectors said, "Hats off to Virat Kohli for the way he

played. We have to start looking towards the future. The selection committee and the Board felt Kohli is future captaincy material."

As a result, he was appointed the vice-captain of the Indian team for the Asia Cup 2012, held in Bangladesh.

Kohli was in good form, yet again scoring the highest runs in the tournament. Even though the Indian team did not make it to the finals, Kohli set several records, including the highest individual score against Pakistan in ODIs (183 runs).

Over the next few months, however, he did not score well. The pressure to perform again started to rise, but Kohli never lost his cool. He saw each innings as a way to learn and improve himself. He realised that he found it difficult to bat well against fast bowlers, so he started

practising even harder, and tried to improve his batting techniques.

By the time the Australian Test Tour of India began in February 2013, Kohli said he was "hungry for this series", after his mediocre form over the last few series. All his

passion to win came to the fore, and he made significant contributions to the team in every match. As a result, Australia lost the series 4-0. This cemented Kohli's spot in the Indian Test team.

In December 2014, Kohli was appointed the captain of the Test team for the first time, when MS Dhoni was injured just before India's tour of Australia. He surpassed all expectations, and scored 115 and 141 during the match. Once again, Kohli's performance was hailed by

many, despite India losing the match. It was called the finest performance they had ever seen in Australia. He took over the position of Test captain officially after the third Test match, when MS Dhoni announced his retirement from Test cricket. Kohli made a total of 692

runs in the series, which was the highest by any Indian against Australia in Test matches.

After this, Kohli focused once again on ODIs. This was a stressful time, as the ICC Cricket World Cup was coming up soon, and India wanted to retain the trophy they had won in 2011.

In the first few matches of the World Cup, the team won all the matches in their group, with Kohli contributing

to several partnerships, and scoring well on his own. However, in the next few matches, he was not able to score, and was dismissed, scoring as low as three and one in the quarter-final and semi-final. India was out of the race for the World Cup.

Kohli faced a lot of criticism from disappointed fans. His bad form continued for the next few months, but he never gave up. With the support of his family and his team, Virat kept his focus. He not only worked on his cricket practice, but also on his overall fitness.

Finally during the Sri Lanka Test tour later in the year, he was back in top form. India won the series 2-1. The series was also Kohli's first series win as the Test captain. After this, he led the Test team once again to defeat South Africa 3-0, which helped India climb to number 2 on the ICC Test rankings. In 2017, MS Dhoni decided to step down as captain of the limited-overs matches as well. Virat stepped up as captain, and has shown great promise in leading the team in ODIs as well.

Thus, Kohli emerged as not only one of the best ODI and Test batsmen in India, but also a very capable and inspiring cricket team captain. His calibre was recognised

in 2017 by the Wisden Cricketers' Almanac, which named him the Leading Cricketer in the world. This highly reputable award was started in 2003, and he is the third Indian cricketer to win, after Virender Sehwag and Sachin Tendulkar.

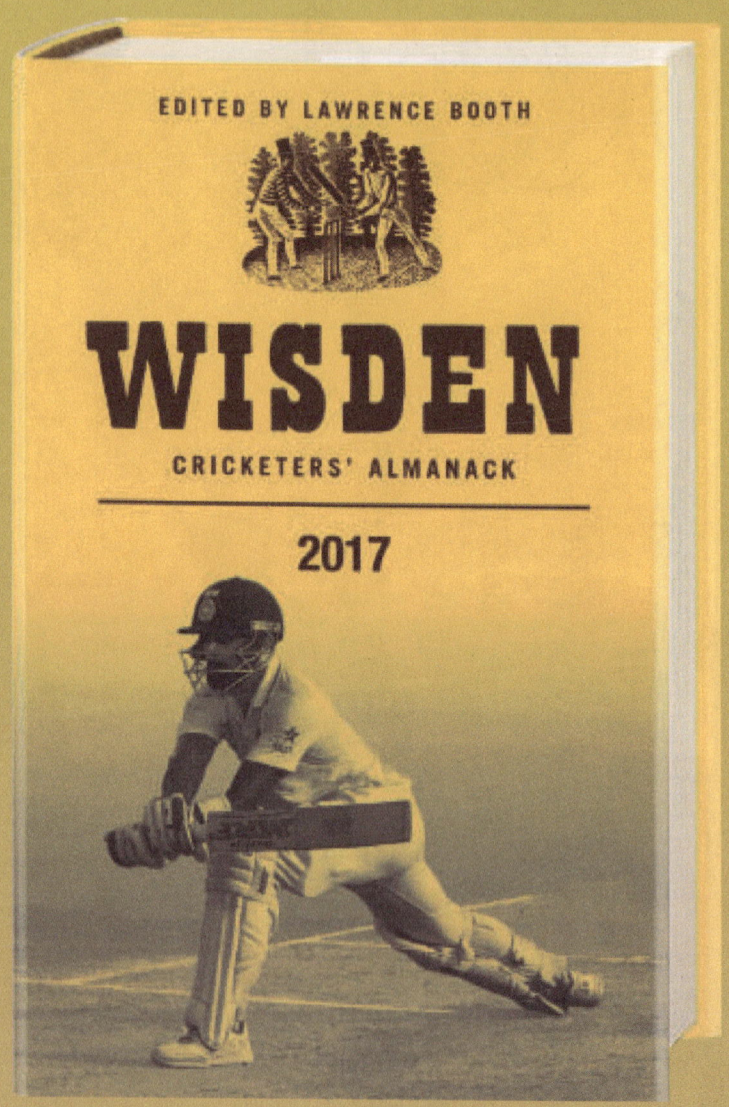

He has shown his talent not just while playing for the Indian team, but also in the IPL matches. Soon after his U-19 World Cup victory, Kohli was picked by the IPL team Royal Challengers Bangalore. He continues to play for the side even today, and as the captain, he has led the team to many victories.

Personal Strengths and Overcoming Challenges

As a cricketer, Kohli's greatest strength is the passion he has for the game. He is an aggressive, attacking player, and at the same time he has a very strong technique. He usually plays as a middle-order batsman, and is comfortable playing

a wide range of shots. He is known for his commitment, focus and confidence. He is also very level headed and mature especially during pressure situations.

Besides being one of the best batsmen in the world, Kohli is also a very good fielder. Since he has also been practising his bowling, he is more and more being seen as

an all-rounder. Kohli's interest in sports is not limited to cricket. He is also a co-owner of the FC Goa team in the Indian Soccer League, and the UAE Royals Team in the International Premier Tennis League.

Early on in his career, Kohli's on-field competitiveness often came across as overly aggressive. He had the reputation of being arrogant and often got into arguments with players and umpires. However, many former cricketers support his aggression on the field, and link it to his competitive spirit. Kohli himself says that while the pressure of the game can make it difficult to control his reactions, he makes it a point to never cross the limit. Over the years he has matured immensely and has learnt to control his reactions better.

Kohli has faced many ups and downs in his career so far. However, he has always met his troubles head-on and has eventually come out of them stronger. The basis of this positive attitude lay in his younger days. At the beginning of his career, when he was still playing for the Delhi team, his

father was his biggest support. However, after his father's death, his family faced some very tough times. The family faced a lot of financial problems, especially since their family business was not doing well. Nonetheless, they faced the challenge together as a family. They moved to

a rented house, and struggled to make sure that not only were their own needs met but that Kohli also continued to get the support he needed to continue with his upcoming cricket career. Those days of hardship shaped Kohli into the man he is today and helped him stay focused on his priorities. The never-say-die attitude and the belief that through hard work one can overcome all challenges has stayed with him.

Kohli has also shown his interest in philanthropy, by setting up a foundation called the 'Virat Kohli Foundation' (VKF) in 2013. The VKF aims to help underprivileged children and raises funds for them with particular focus on their education and healthcare.

Personal Life

Virat Kohli married popular Indian film actress Anushka Sharma in a secret ceremony on December 11, 2017 in Tuscany, Italy. The two first met at the shoot for a TV commercial in 2013 and dated for almost 4 long years before tying the knot.

Since he started playing for the Indian National Cricket Team, Virat Kohli has set many records and received many awards. Here are a few important ones:

- Arjuna Award for Cricket 2013 (awarded by Ministry of Youth Affairs and Sports, Government of India, to recognise and to appreciate outstanding achievement in national sports)

- Ranked no. 1 in ICC Rankings for T20 (as of 2016)

- Ranked no. 2 in ICC Rankings for ODIs (as of 2016)

- ICC ODI Cricketer of the Year 2012

- BCCI International Cricketer of the Year 2011-12 and 2014-15

- Second batsman in the world to score over 1,000 ODI runs for 4 consecutive years (after Saurav Ganguly)

- Fastest batsman in the world to reach 7,000 ODI runs (in 169 matches)

Records, Awards and Recognition

- Fastest Indian ODI century (100 runs in 52 balls)
- Fastest batsman to score 1,000 runs in T20
- Most 50s in T20 Internationals (16)
- Most runs in a single tournament for both ICC World T20 and IPL

Timeline

- **1988** Born in New Delhi

- **1998** Joins the newly formed West Delhi Cricket Academy

- **2002** Captain, Delhi U-15 Team for the Polly Umrigar Trophy

- **2006** Member, India Under-19 Squad; debuts in first class cricket for Delhi; father passes away in November

- **2007** Debuts in T20 cricket, with the Interstate T20 Championship

- **2008** As captain of the U-19 Indian Team wins the U-19 World Cup in Malaysia; Gets picked for the IPL T20 team Royal Challengers Bangalore; International ODI debut in the Indian tour of Sri Lanka

- **2009** Leading run scorer at the Emerging Players Tournament in Australia; scores first ODI century against Sri Lanka in Eden Gardens, Kolkata

- **2011** Indian team wins the ICC World Cup; Test debut against West Indies

Timeline

- **2012** Maiden Test century against Australia; ICC ODI Cricketer of the Year Award

- **2013** Arjuna Award for Sports, awarded by Government of India

- **2014** Captain, Indian Test Team

- **2015** His first series win as Test Captain

- **2016** Record for highest number of runs in T20 format in a single season (973 runs in 16 innings)

- **2017** Wisden Cricketers' Almanac honours him as Leading Cricketer in the World.

Group Activity

- Pick one sportsperson and prepare a presentation about them. Remember to find out the following information: What sport do they play? How long have they played it? What awards have they received?
- Find out more about the different formats of cricket. What is the difference between a Test match and an ODI?
- Divide the class into teams and organise a 5-over match.

Class Discussion

- Why are sports important for us? What is the importance of sports in our lives?
- Debate on the topic: 'Sports should be given as much importance as studies in school'.

Activities

Questions

1. Where was Virat Kohli born?
2. Who gave him the nickname 'Cheeku'?
3. Why did he change his school in Class 9?
4. Where did Virat Kohli first learn proper batting techniques?
5. In which tournament did Virat Kohli lead the Delhi Under-15 Team?
6. Why was the first-class match against Karnataka significant in Virat Kohli's life?
7. Who was the Captain of the Indian U-19 Squad in 2008? Which tournament did they win?
8. Where and when did Virat Kohli first get to play for the Indian National Team?
9. What did Virat Kohli do when he could not score in a number of matches?
10. Why was Virat Kohli fined by the match referee in Sydney in 2011?
11. Which IPL team does Virat Kohli play for?
12. When was Virat Kohli awarded the Arjuna Award and by whom?
13. What does the VKF do?
14. Why was Virat Kohli made the captain of the Indian Test team in Australia in 2014?